HELLERTOWN AREA LIBRARY
409 Constitution Avenue
Hellertown, PA 18055
610-838-8381

NO CROWN REQUIRED

Raising a Confident, Courageous, and Compassionate Daughter

www.mascotbooks.com

*No Crown Required: Raising a Confident,
Courageous, and Compassionate Daughter*

©2018 Susan Kay Wyatt. All Rights Reserved. No part of this publication may be reproduced, stored in a retrieval system or transmitted in any form by any means electronic, mechanical, or photocopying, recording or otherwise without the permission of the author.

I have tried to recreate events, locales, and conversations from my memories of them. I may have changed some identifying characteristics and details, such as physical properties, occupations, places of residence, and names in order to maintain subject anonymity. My memories are my own, and I have recalled the stories recorded here to the best of my ability.

For more information, please contact:
Mascot Books
620 Herndon Parkway #320
Herndon, VA 20170
info@mascotbooks.com

CPSIA Code: PBANG0518A
Library of Congress Control Number: 2018904160
ISBN-13: 978-1-64307-072-8

Printed in the United States

No Crown Required

Raising a Confident, Courageous, and Compassionate Daughter

SUSAN KAY WYATT

FOR ELIZABETH AND MY MOM

TABLE OF CONTENTS

A NOTE FROM THE AUTHOR — xi

INTRODUCTION — 1

Flashback—The Ohio State University Vocal Performance Department, Dr. Hickfang's Voice Studio — 3

PROLOGUE — 7

Flashback—Ugly — 12

CHAPTER 1: Beauty — 15

Flashback—The Miss America Pageant, Backstage Swimsuit Competition — 23

CHAPTER 2: Swimsuit — 27

Flashback— My Hand-Me-Down Evening Gown — 37

CHAPTER 3: Evening Gown — 41

Flashback—Miss America Talent Competition — 48

CHAPTER 4: Talent — 51

Flashback—Interview, Atlantic City Hotel — 57

CHAPTER 5: Interview 61

Flashback—Ohio Stadium Halftime Show 70

CHAPTER 6: The Bad and the Ugly 73

CHAPTER 7: The Good 79

Flashback—Being Crowned Miss Ohio 84

CHAPTER 8: And Finally... 87

CHAPTER 9: ...Wrap It Up in a Bow! 91

ACKNOWLEDGMENTS 97

A NOTE FROM THE AUTHOR

The launching of my debut book feels intoxicating to me. It's the natural progression in my creative and well-examined life. My obsession with self-help, healing, spirituality, psychology, the sisterhood of women, and positive parenting has led me to this place. The #MeToo and #TimesUp movements, especially the Miss America shake-up, have gifted me the perfect timing to finally get my message of heart-centered connection—and the necessity of healing our damaged sisterhood—out into the world.

Look for my next book *Skip the Princess, Raise the Queen: Daily Wisdom Practices.* Coming soon.

XO, SK

INTRODUCTION

Not long after I came home from the Miss America competition, I moved on to the next entertainment job that crossed my path. That led to me entering into a five-year personal relationship that wasn't about me.

I lost myself in someone else's world, where I wasn't encouraged to continue to pursue my singing career. I was surrounded by people who weren't my biggest fans. It was as if they didn't really see me. I began to feel that I must not be good enough, and my self-esteem began to spiral. I was even convinced that I had changed my mind about what I wanted to do with my life. Deep down, I knew better.

I kept thinking about my life of music performance work leading up to that point. I found myself talking about my journey in the Miss America program. We were on our way to an event, and my now ex-husband was driving. I was talking about how I cracked the code of the pageant and what it took to make that happen. "No one wants to hear about that," he said. "You have to stop talking about that." I said nothing after that. I felt frustrated and ashamed.

But it occurred to me that I wasn't bragging or boasting or living in the past. Because it wasn't the pageant I was talking about. It was the girl who cracked the code. It was the girl who had fire and focus. It was the girl who overcame obstacles and learned to improve herself. It was the girl who knew who she was and what she wanted to do since birth. It was the girl who believed in her dreams and everyone else's too. She was courageous and confident. People loved and believed in her. She was unstoppable. But at that moment, she was nowhere to be found.

I wanted her back. I wanted to be the girl who cracked the code again. I thought if I could do what I did in that couple of years with the pageant, I could surely do it again with the next big thing. Knowing what I was capable of, not being her didn't make any sense.

Fast-forward thirty years to my life with a sixteen-year-old daughter and a husband who is my biggest fan in every way. I have struggled over the years with that negative voice that got stuck in my head telling me no one cares what I have to say. With the help of a loving mentor and the love and support of family and friends, I finally kicked it to the curb.

This book is for that daring, determined, dynamic girl.

That girl is me.

That girl is you.

Flashback

The Ohio State University Vocal Performance Department, Dr. Hickfang's Voice Studio

It was the fall of my junior year in 1985 at The Ohio State University when my voice professor, Dr. Hickfang, told me that he was a judge for the Miss Ohio Pageant that summer and proudly announced that I should enter the next year and, in his humble opinion, could win the thing! I'll never forget that moment of excitement and fear. It was as if he had dropped a bomb on my life. I can still feel that pit in my stomach.

I was at a point in my life where I was getting lost but wasn't fully aware of it yet. My obsession with an egomaniac boyfriend and partying was taking a toll on me. I struggled with relationships with other girls who bullied me behind my back. My secret struggle with plummeting self-esteem and depression defied outer appearances to the contrary. I wasn't sure where I fit in to the performance career I had dreamed of.

Performing onstage was second nature to me. That was my comfort zone and my forte. But that was not all this pageant was about. I remembered watching the Miss America Pageant on TV as a little girl and being in awe of the beautiful, smart, and savvy contestants. But I never seriously imagined being on that stage myself.

I knew I could work hard and handle the swimsuit competition. Evening gown didn't seem like brain surgery. But the interview and onstage pop question? I wasn't in the know about politics and world news. I didn't know where I stood on important issues. I wasn't a fully self-realized human. That would prove to be my biggest challenge and eventually my ultimate triumph.

What I did know for sure? I was embarking on some unknown adventure and needed all the help I could get.

PROLOGUE

*I*t's a girl!

Hearing those words for me was the most exciting yet terrifying news. My life flashed before my eyes, just like you hear happens before someone dies. Every moment of triumph and heartbreak flooded my mind. How would I be able to mentor this precious life to handle it all better than I did? I was excited about the challenge and the honor of the task ahead. I consumed books on raising children with healthy self-esteem and was mesmerized by it all. I attracted into my life moms and experts who helped me understand positive parenting. And I found the inner strength, wisdom, and love that would be the key to raising this amazing girl I call my daughter.

Women. Society pits us against each other, and we allow it. Competition, comparison, perfection, and the endless struggle for power rule our world.

Beauty pageants place all these things front and center in a shiny, sparkly, primitive bloodbath that evokes the strongest feelings of fear, self-loathing, and inadequacy in the hearts and solar plexuses of women around the world. I know firsthand, for I have been there and have known deep down for some time that there is a reconciliation of what this truly means, why it is important, and how we can go forward together.

I went to the Miss America Pageant as Miss Ohio 1988. Of all the things I am in this world, people seem to be most fascinated when they find out I held that title and went to Miss America. It's the strangest thing. Like a car wreck where people rubberneck to see the carnage. They just can't help but look. They want to know all about it. "What was it really like?"

It was a double-edged sword. It seemed to be impressive to most, an official validation of my "beauty," yet the stigma of being a "pageant bimbo" was unbearable for me.

We live in a competitive world. This book is for all the women who have been brave enough to put it all on the line and be judged by some impossible standard. And for those who wished they had tried. And for those who couldn't imagine being good enough to even think about it. And for those who went on to do great things in the world because of or in spite of it. It's even for those of you who wouldn't consider it in a million years. Because life is the pageant. To win, we have to show up as our best selves.

Showing up as our best selves requires the tools to make that happen. Even with the dedication, love, and support I got from my parents, I didn't get quite all of those tools growing up. It's what I *did* get from my pageant experience that changed my life and gave me the tools I strive to give my daughter. It's about that mysterious thing called self-esteem and the confidence to be who we are and love who we are.

There are four areas of competition required to win the crown. They are swimsuit, evening gown, talent, and interview. Each of these areas of competition applies to real life and is necessary to achieve success, happiness, fulfillment, and balance.

As crazy as it sounds, the pageant people aren't completely off their nut. There are just some major tweaks to what it all really means in today's world of diverse beauty and talent, in a world where women are inundated, saturated, and degraded with a pop culture that is demeaning and devoid of substance. Yes, in all of that, there is a basic formula, and you don't need to enter a pageant or wear a crown to utilize these tools.

It needs to be said that the Miss America Pageant, with all its flaws, is not merely a "beauty" pageant. It's a scholarship pageant and has awarded millions of dollars to help thousands of women pay for their college education. The women I met, competed with, and befriended during my short pageant stint are some of the smartest, kindest, down-to-earth, most successful people I have ever known. They continue to inspire me and everyone around them as they share their talents, make a difference in their chosen fields, and give back to make the world a better place.

This book is part of a healing journey of a long-damaged sisterhood. It's a cry for ending the infighting of women and girls. It's an understanding of the competitiveness, self-doubt, low self-esteem, and pain that is at the core of every bitch who crosses our paths and why we are bitches ourselves.

It's part of the legacy I am passing on to my daughter. It's wisdom I have been sharing with her since she was born so that she will grow up to be an empowered, beautiful, inspired, loving, confident, strategic leader and a positive force in the world.

Being a contestant in the Miss America Pageant is a brief part of my "Wicky Wacky" life! It's a two-year snapshot in time. I was not a pageant girl. I was a performer who was looking to get exposure to further my career. What I got was not what I expected and way more than I bargained for. Those two years had such a profound impact on me that they changed the way I show up in the world. They revealed to me that inspiring, encouraging, and empowering girls and women are a huge part of my life path, a path that took me another two decades and the birth of my daughter to begin to understand. And even as I write this, I smile at the ever-unfolding complexity of that understanding.

If you are the mom of a daughter, like me, you know firsthand what you want for your daughter's life. You want her to know everything that no one told you! You want her to stand with other women and not against them. You don't have to have a daughter to want that for all the women in your life. We all finally get the "information" in our forties (some even later), and we sure could have used it in grade school.

The truth is, if you give your daughter the tools to be confident and love herself for who she is, she will have a real shot at achieving her dreams, especially if she sees the best in other people and holds that vision for them, knowing that there is enough success and prosperity for everyone. After all, when I took a poll of moms asking what they wanted for their daughters, it was happiness. Life doesn't get much happier than manifesting our dreams.

I don't look back on this time to live in the past. I look back to celebrate how far I have come and share the wisdom of each life lesson. I know that when we cultivate compassion, courage, and confidence in ourselves and others, we all win.

No more bloodbath. No crowns required. But you may want to fasten your seatbelt.

Because life *is* the pageant.

Here we go.

Flashback

Ugly

It was the day after I won the Miss Ohio Pageant. I was fresh from a hot bath my mom had drawn for me in our hotel room following an after party the night before. I felt frail and small. I felt humbled and scared for what was ahead. I was in a sleepless haze of afterglow. I was just 22 years old.

The board members gathered at the estate-like home of a woman who would become a beloved friend. There was a shakeup with the pageant directors resulting in a change of guard. They brought in a man who supposedly knew how to get Miss Ohio ready. He was flamboyant and colorful, and I shall refer to him as the Miss Ohio Guy.

A majestic mahogany dining room table and chairs and wallpaper with light-blue ribbons would be forever etched in my mind. My parents and I sat around that table anticipating the support and wisdom that would take me on this next leg of my journey.

The Miss Ohio Guy marched me to the powder room mirror and assessed the dire situation. "Your eyebrows are too thick. Your lips are too thin," he said as he proceeded to take a lip liner to the outer rim, creating a horrific clown-like appearance. "Your face is too round." Pumpkin Face became a nickname that still grinds my stomach to this day. "Dark contouring must be done." They had just crowned their winner, and I wasn't pretty. This was new for me.

Then, one month before Atlantic City: "Miss Ohio's picture just hit the papers, and whoa, is she ugly!"

The morning radio guys were howling with laughter while my roommate was in the kitchen having her morning coffee, getting ready for work. For the first time in her life, she called in to a radio show to defend her beloved friend. I became comedy fodder during drive time for every radio listening Columbus, Ohio, citizen on their way to work.

A not-so-flattering photo taken by a newspaper reporter was released to the media, and I was presented with a box filled with autograph pads with that same photo on it! And so it went. I seemed to be in an alternate universe where I was ugly, and it was quite sporting to let me know it.

It was that week that I would see the glamorous headshots of all the girls I would meet in Atlantic City. I had a sinking feeling that I was out of my league. That feeling was new for me too and the beginning of a crisis of self-esteem.

I began to think that maybe I was just not that pretty, even though I knew differently deep inside. It would also be the beginning of a lifetime quest to find a good photographer and the self-love and confidence required to get a good shot. Which I eventually did.

CHAPTER 1
Beauty

The yearly parade of Barbie Doll clones on a stage does not represent who Miss America is. There is no way that the beautiful girls on that pageant stage represent us all.

When I was pitching my book to a publisher at a workshop, a woman came up to me afterward. She was short, older, with light-brown skin and an accent I couldn't place. She was lovely in her flowing garment of multicolored fabric and glowing with a beauty and sweetness that was magical. "The Miss America Pageant makes me sick to my stomach," she said to me. I said, "I know that feeling well. You don't like my book idea?"

"No, I love it. Please write your book." We embraced. She was beautiful. She saw herself in my eyes and I in hers.

One of the biggest issues emanating from the entertainment industry and pageant world is the obsession with a certain standard of physical appearance that is considered beautiful. What is worse, it has been given the power to set the tone or standard for all of us. That's simply crazy.

As an intuitive, conscious, empathic, and highly observant human being and an expert in seeing beauty in the world, I protest. So much does this concept bother me that I have spent the last several years since the birth of my daughter trying to make sense of it all as we strive to move forward as human beings with infinite potential, beyond the skin-deep perceptions of this mindlessly vapid pop culture realm we occupy.

While indeed there is so much more to us, we do need to live and conduct business in this material world. We need to find the truth of our own beauty. Own it. Love it. Release it to the world at large. We need to get a handle on this beauty thing once and for all because the idea of it is not going away.

We live in a high-definition world. It's not of our choosing. But it is reality for us and our daughters. The look that defines the current standard of beauty in this century has been perpetuated by Hollywood starlets on the silver screen. It escalated with Barbie, Playboy Bunnies, Victoria's Secret models, and now pop stars. Most of these images used to be confined to magazines you had to purchase. But for quite a while now, we've been seeing it all on our small screens that we are addicted to checking all day long, and larger than life on our HD supersize screens in our living rooms. We do not get to choose this either, because if you don't watch an actual show featuring this kind of content, random commercials happily

> *Ignorance is not bliss. Be aware of the media, but don't overconsume it. Don't pretend that it doesn't exist, because we can't escape it.*

feed us these images daily. Don't watch TV? You can see these images on billboards, buses, and street ads. Unless you plan on hiding out under a rock, you will be processing this concept of beauty in one way or another.

Societal beauty standards and our bombardment of these images is a major discussion that has to happen with our daughters. Whether or not we feel it should be important in our lives, it just is. As much as we say not to compare ourselves to others, we do. And every woman has a need to know that she is beautiful. Because she is. It begins when they're babies. And even if you saturate their brains with supportive positive messages, when they hit their teens, it blows up in traumatic and dramatic ways. I know because I raised my daughter to love who she is on the inside and out, and still, when she hit her teens, she had issues with what she looked like. The truth is that we women as moms are still dealing with those same feelings. Our daughters give us the chance to heal that within ourselves and be the example for them to navigate it all.

The first step is to talk to our daughters. Not just once, but all the time. Talk to them about all of it because they are seeing it, feeling it, and thinking about it. This requires ongoing conversation, and not just as moms but as sisters. Sisters on the path supporting each other. And we can be both because our daughters need us as parents and as lifelong friends. We can only tackle this as a sisterhood.

Taking the media out of the equation, why are we

obsessed with beauty? Because we are visual beings, and seeing something that is beautiful in our eyes brings us great joy and pleasure. Who gets to decide what and who is beautiful? We do. And each person, for the most part, has a different opinion of what real outer beauty is.

The truth that we know is that real beauty emanates from the inside. It is an energy of love, joy, and peace. Beauty is revealed in kindness, humor, confidence, and passion. Beauty sees beauty in all things and all people. Beauty lives and loves life. Beauty is the art of loving oneself enough to see and feel the beauty in ourselves. And from that self-love, seeing it in the world and sharing it with the world. We can't help it. It just spills out in great waves and attracts beauty unto itself. A beautiful idea and quite poetic, yes? It is truth. But it's not always easy to understand.

Have you known people who are not traditionally physically attractive, yet everyone is in love with them and attracted to them? I have. And on the other hand, we've all seen a physically beautiful woman who appears ugly because of what is going on inside her heart, her brain, or her world. While mostly we want to bitch slap her, what she really needs is a big hug.

We all need a big hug. Not only that, we need to talk about all of this with one another and our daughters. Because not talking about it doesn't make it go away. I talk about it all with my daughter so she can understand all the feelings she will most certainly experience in this physical world.

We each get a barrage of constant messages that

settle deep into our subconscious, where they marinate. Everything we've heard goes in. We know this is true, yet we participate in the madness. And it doesn't end there. It continues throughout our childhood when the messages get cemented so deeply it takes massive therapy or a good shaman to excavate, extrapolate, and exorcise the muckety-muck.

> *Have the conversation with the girl in the mirror. That girl is you. I believe we should all practice self-forgiveness: "I am sorry; please forgive me; thank you; I love you." This comes from a Hawaiian practice of healing reconciliation and forgiveness called* Ho'oponopono. *Loving others begins with loving yourself.*

This madness all matters because we, as grown-ups, are *still* dealing with old messages. And we are giving our daughters messages about their value as human beings too.

To stop the madness, we must do the work to heal ourselves so that we can be fully present to give our daughters what they need to survive the onslaught and thrive. Every tool in this toolbox we must master the use of ourselves, because our daughters learn by what they observe.

All this is critical in learning to manage the bombardment of images and messages we receive. It's the ongoing conversations we have with our daughters about it that will give them the confidence and clarity they will need to deflect what comes at them and make smart decisions for their own happiness.

A parent tells a girl she is the most beautiful girl in

the world, but the parent forgets to mention that there are other beautiful girls out there too. Imagine how unequipped that girl is to handle the reality. Alternatively, a parent told me she would never tell her daughter that she was beautiful because her mom told her that, and she didn't want her daughter obsessing over that. I can't imagine how someone feels if her own mom won't tell her she is beautiful.

> *Sit down with your daughter and have the conversation about all the different ways beauty shows up in the world. Always share the joy of diversity with her. It can't be overstated.*

How about this? I tell my daughter she is the most beautiful girl in the world to me because she is mine and I do good work. Ha! We also look at other girls and notice their beauty. And we process feelings of envy or sparks of jealousy together. Mostly we applaud and celebrate all the diverse beauty we encounter every day. It's much more fun that way.

When my daughter was a kindergartener, I took the message of *The Twelve Gifts of Birth* (a book by Charlene Costanzo) into her classroom. I produced music for each of the gifts and was excited to share these powerful tools with the little ones. I will never forget the day I talked about beauty with the girls.

We sat in a circle. I had them look at one another and notice how different they all were. There was curly and straight hair, black, brown, and blonde; all shades of skin. Oh, and the different shapes and colors of their eyes! Each girl agreed that all of them were unique. I then had them look at one another and think of their moms, dads, or puppies. Smiles and love emanated from them. It was clear that everyone looked happy and pretty. Then I had them think of something bad and make the ugliest face they could muster. How quickly a group of beautiful little girls turned ugly. It fascinated them.

Then I asked them, "If another girl is beautiful, does that mean that you are not?" They mostly didn't know, but some said yes. You should have seen them when I explained that someone else being pretty does not negate anyone else's beauty. **There is enough beauty, love, and happiness for everyone.** I saw them shift with my own eyes. This is the power of having the conversation.

The conversations must begin when they are little. And look out for puberty. I was naming and proclaiming that my daughter would never go through the awkward stage. Of course, I was wrong. One look at a junior high class anywhere will make anyone uncomfortable! They need us then more than ever.

They are headed into the crazy world of their sexuality. This is a critical point when they can lose interest in their gifts and talents and become obsessed with sex, social media,

> *Pay attention to what you and your daughter are saying and doing when it comes to beauty. Always be aware of the way you present your attitude about beauty to your daughter—because if she learns to have a healthy attitude toward beauty, it will be from you.*

popularity, and a myriad of substances to cope. ***Girls can get lost pretty quickly. It's a wild ride, and if they aren't internally validated as smart and beautiful, talented, loved, and treasured, they will look for validation outside of themselves. I know of what I speak because I went through all of it!***

We must get the beauty thing under control because we have lots of other things to talk about that will make for a life of balance and happiness. Free their consciousness to focus on their unique gifts and big dreams. To make them come true, they need to be able to show up as their best selves in a very competitive world.

Our daughters need to be in a place of clarity within themselves, of confidence, compassion, and courage.

Being beautiful would just be a given.

Flashback

The Miss America Pageant, Backstage Swimsuit Competition

Just got backstage from walking that long, sleek, shiny black runway in my virtuous, virginal-white one-piece supersuit—which, by the way, was the official Miss America–approved swimsuit at the time. The Miss Ohio Guy had found his way to my locker to urgently notify me that my boobs didn't look big enough onstage. Now, mind you, I had a pushup bra and a pound of padding already locked and loaded in that thing. What to do? His solution was to take my gym socks and put them in there too. And I did.

It was too late for judging the preliminary, of course, but if I made it to the top ten, I'd be mega-super-boob ready! We all had to go back out onstage for them to announce the preliminary talent and swimsuit winners for the night. My boobs stuck out so far, I kept running into people and doorways. I could not steer those things. But I smiled my way through the group swimsuit musical number, where I was safely hidden in the back row, mortified of losing my gym socks.

Miss Georgia snagged the swimsuit prize that night. Instead of Miss America White, she wore a hot-pink suit with no padding. She didn't have giant boobs. She was gorgeous, of course, a natural beauty, but she was no lovelier than any other girl on that stage.

I remember thinking, "If only I had worn that red suit that looked so perfect on me." The suit that won me the swimsuit trophy at my local pageant. My boobs are the perfect size and proportion for my body. I knew that then. I wish I could have trusted myself. And then came "Why didn't I work out more?" I was beating myself up inside.

Years later I came across a picture of me walking down that runway that I thought at the time was terrible. I now have it hanging in my office to remind me how crazy I was to think that my body wasn't beautiful enough. I love that photo, and I love telling my younger self, "You rocked that runway."

CHAPTER 2

Swimsuit

*I*n the current state of the pageant world, you must have the perfect rock-hard hourglass-yet-size-two figure with big boobs; long, sleek legs; and the right amount of thigh gap. Strap on a pair of four-inch heels, glide down a long runway after tackling some steep stairs, and top it off with a turn where your ass gets evaluated for tightness and form. Your stomach? So flat it connects to your spine.

Where the pageant and current culture fail us is that only one body type is celebrated. That body type, while beautiful, doesn't represent all women. And that is a legit reason for the pageants to get a bad rap.

In real life, the swimsuit competition isn't about swimsuit. It's about fitness, health, discipline, and self-esteem. It's something that affects all other areas of our lives. How we feel about the way we look is a huge factor in how we feel about ourselves. How healthy and energetic we are affects our ability to go and do what we need to do in this world to be strong and endure everything that life throws at us. Getting a handle on this is an essential tool for our success.

Where does actual swimsuit happen in real life? It's called summer. And we as women have to decide whether we're going to sit on the sidelines all covered up and hide or get out there and have fun! And if you are a mom, you will have plenty of opportunities, from the backyard kiddie pool to summer vacations on the beach, to wear that swimsuit.

How do we raise our own self-esteem about our bodies and raise our girls to love theirs? How do we help our girls be their best without making them obsessed with comparing their physical beauty to that of other women? Well, it starts with us showing them the way. We have to heal our wounds about our bodies and love ourselves for the "model" we were given.

There are so many different body types. Comparison happens. Saying that it's bad to compare or thinking that we as women shouldn't doesn't mean that comparison won't happen. An ongoing conversation about our bodies is important.

I talk to my daughter about how I feel about my body and how important my fitness is to me. When I was younger, it was all about weighing myself. I have finally turned that corner, but it still rears its ugly head. When I'm not feeling so hot about myself, I tell her that too. It's important to know that we all have good days and bad. And she can give me crap when I get too obsessive. Which I do. It's mostly a direct result of being a stage performer and being under the scrutiny that comes with being photographed, which means having to see photos of myself, most of them unflattering. I have been honest with her about that because she is too smart. I also tell her how beautiful her body is. I always tell her that she is my best work. And I say, "You are welcome," which makes her laugh.

She wasn't always confident. One summer she went to an art conservatory camp where she got to experience several disciplines, from drawing to script writing to ballet. Standing next to the thin ballet girls in the mirror was a huge blow. She was thirteen at the time. She also wore the worst long shorts, that made her look dumpy, which she is not. That was the first time she understood dressing for her body. She was amazed at how different she looked in the right clothing. I also told her to never stand next to a ballerina in front of a mirror in a dance studio! I know from experience—it's a real buzzkill.

> *Start slow. Rome wasn't built in a day. If you over-train before you are ready, you will make yourself sick or injure yourself, and your progress would be halted completely.*

It was an important conversation because she was agonizing about it. I couldn't ignore it because she wasn't ignoring it. She didn't like talking about it because she didn't like that icky feeling that she wasn't good enough. We needed to process it together, which we did. We cried, and we laughed. I took her home and put her in front of the mirror and said, "Are you kidding me? Have you seen your gorgeous curves and those gams? And your skin is so beautiful! We're small, curvy girls, and I wouldn't want any other body. Now get rid of those ugly shorts." Whew! Disaster averted. To this day we still have ab and gun contests in that mirror and when caught streaking through the house, we say, "Have you seen this?" Loving our bodies feels so good.

I have always been open about my struggle throughout my life with the ups and downs of my weight, fitness, and body image—none worse than when I turned fifty. I found out it had to do with my hormone levels and that pesky thing called menopause. I felt irritable and depressed. I had stopped working out after hip and knee injuries from six years of martial arts. My favorite clothes didn't fit the same, and I didn't recognize the woman I saw in the mirror. Even though I kept up my pleasant demeanor to the outside world, I was deeply depressed. I lost all interest in my creative endeavors, including my music and finishing writing this book. I lost my mojo! It wasn't good for my marriage either. I would often apologize to my husband and daughter for not being myself. They felt helpless but were supportive.

> *Healthy eating is a lifestyle, not a diet. Find what works for you. Allow yourself time to be naughty too. And when you are having a moment with junk food, own it and enjoy it. "Nothing to see here" is a saying we use in our house. No blame. No shame.*

It was the sisterhood of friends I have in place that would save me. I was telling a mom friend that my physical therapist recommended Pilates. My biggest issue was that Pilates was expensive. She told me about a Groupon for a studio close by. We went together. I'll never forget standing in front of that mirror assessing the damage. My ego was angry, and I felt old and unattractive. But I saw a glimmer of that girl who cracked the code. I made a commitment that day to that girl in the mirror, and I kept it. I knew it was going to take time, and I would have to be compassionate with myself. That was two years ago as I write this book. It was a slow process, but I started to see results more and more. Now I am more lean and fit than I have ever been. I was worth the investment of time and money in Pilates. And when I made a commitment to a monthly payment, the price was more affordable.

Commit to a schedule and keep your appointments with yourself. Buying a monthly package for Pilates, yoga, or any other workout class forces you to do that.

There is an ad campaign for an anti-aging cream that resonates with me: ***Methods, not miracles. If you are in a place where you need to start, just start. Know that it won't happen overnight but little by little, step by step, you have the power to transform any area of your life.*** And once you arrive at your destination, it takes continued discipline to stay there. We all fall short at times. That is where the sisterhood comes in. We can show up together to a workout class or just take power walks together. We can cheer each other on, cry on each other's shoulders, and share resources for health and wellness. If you don't have a close circle of friends, there are amazing communities of women online. I have found the more I reach out, the bigger that supportive group gets.

With recommendations from other women going through the same things, I solved the hormone issue, which gave me back my zest for life. My hormone deficiency was a health issue that was solvable. Listen to your body. Find a physician and health coach who specializes in women's health you can relate to and trust. We go through many phases and changes in life that affect our health and our weight. You are worth figuring out what that is for you.

> *Just start—it's never going to be the perfect time. The perfect time is this moment. It's right now.*

Issues with our bodies don't just happen at fifty. They happen all through our lives for different reasons. Everyone is going through something, so staying out of judgement regarding where other women are on their physical journey is critical. We must remember that we are not alone, nor are our health and fitness struggles something to be ashamed of. Our society does a great job of shaming women. It is up to us to change that narrative. Compassion for one another is an essential part of healing the damaged sisterhood. This is how women get things done. We do it together.

There is beauty in the process of self-acceptance. Just let that soak in. No matter where you are on the physical fitness spectrum or body type, your beauty shines through if you let it. That brings me to celebrating different body types.

On our bike and running route one day, we saw

an elite athlete. Her skin was like dark chocolate. Her body was ripped and cut, and she ran like a gazelle. She was stunning! We were in awe of her. My daughter and I talked about that. At Disneyland we saw a group of high school kids. One girl caught my eye. She was tall and had a thick body. She was magical and oozed confidence. Did she have a ballet body? Nope. She was beautiful. I have a close friend who is curvy, to say the least. No matter whether her weight is up or down, she looks gorgeous! Big boobs! Tiny waist. Major booty! She is so hot that she turns heads everywhere she goes. Does she look like a ballet dancer? Nope. Do any of these women look like my daughter and me? Nope. Are they attractive? Oh my, yes. Do we love them and applaud them? Yes!

Don't forget to reward yourself as you reach your goals! They are important milestones in your self-growth journey and should be celebrated.

Because of social media, bullying and body shaming have become a blood sport with dire consequences. What if we just mind our own business and work on being our best selves? If we stay in our heart space and out of judgement, we won't feel the need to tear other people down to make ourselves feel good. Women who need to do this have low self-esteem and probably someone shaming them in their lives, or they are witnessing it. It is a learned behavior. Our daughters are learning from us as moms, other family members, their friends, and everything they are exposed to. This is a high-priority item that involves knowing who is influencing your daughter and having the conversations.

My daughter grew up watching me go on runs and head to the gym. We took martial arts for six years and earned our black belts together. Most recently I found a passion for Pilates. Whatever I do I am committed, and she can see the results in my appearance and my happiness factor. We also love to take hikes or ride bikes as a family. And my husband is a triathlete who inspires us daily.

My husband and I were worried that our daughter would never enjoy an active lifestyle. She has always been a serious bookworm and artist and didn't like any kind of exercise. She tried soccer and found no joy. She had a love-hate relationship with martial arts but endured six years to earn her black belt. It was basketball for a hot minute, but no love found there either. She eventually discovered conditioning at her school. It would be a charismatic and fun trainer who sealed the deal. Now she spends every day after school in the training room and outdoor killer circuits. She discovered track and loves pole vaulting and long jump. None of these things will be her career. She does it for the energy release, fitness, and fun. She also found a tribe of girls in that conditioning room with common goals.

> *Find your fitness friends! Our daughters need to find friends who support one another in all aspects of life. It took my daughter years to find her peeps in the training room—but once you do, you'll never look back.*

After she spent a week feeling crappy because her

coach was out of town, I picked her up from conditioning. She had a huge smile on her face, and she was glowing. "Mom, I now know that I can't function without working out." With a big smile on my face, I high-fived her. Her decision. Her realization. Happiness! Whew! That was a great mom moment for me.

I don't stay fit for my husband or for any other people. I do it for me. When I'm strong and fit, I feel sexy. When I love what I look like, I feel confident and beautiful. It brings me joy. Some people will say men like some extra padding, and some say otherwise. I think everyone is attracted to different things. My husband loves me no matter my weight or fitness. And he never comments about that. He only ever says I am beautiful and is smart enough and kind enough not to engage in critiquing my figure. I had an ex who always wanted to buy me big boobs. He is an EX. My husband loves my body exactly as it is. Let's just say he responds well to my confidence. And the adoring relationship we share is not lost on my daughter.

Find physical activities that you love and make them a part of your daily life. Change it up. Get creative. Whatever you need to do, get it done. Call on your girlfriends! Make it fun! I don't have to tell you how amazing it feels to be fit or how good it feels to

> *Gear is everything, starting with the right shoes. That is a tip from my husband. As you work out, your feet are taking the biggest hit. You don't have to spend a fortune, but treat them right, or you could halt your progress by injuring yourself.*

put good food into your body and wear that little black dress, your sexy jeans, or, dare I say...a swimsuit!

If we don't have systems in place that ensure we're fit and healthy for life, we unnecessarily put ourselves in very stressful periods of time. Weddings, vacations, proms, black-tie events, and the dreaded class reunions send women into a diet frenzy that isn't healthy—not to mention the blow to our self-esteem.

What if we raise our daughters to be ready for anything? What if we decided to live our lives to be ready for anything? ***Pay attention, listen, and have the conversation. Shoot straight. Be honest, and they will be too. The behavior you model is the behavior they will learn.***

Your body is your temple. Learn to love it and nurture it. Give yourself that gift. You are worth it. And your happiness depends on it.

When you don't feel you have the courage to be your best self, push forward. Always. Don't forget that your daughter is waiting for you to lead by example, so be there for her. She's paying attention, I promise.

Loving your body requires compassion. It takes courage and determination to facilitate positive change. Confidence will follow.

No crown required.

Flashback

My Hand-Me-Down Evening Gown

My first step on the pageant journey was signing up for a local pageant in the town of Pickerington, Ohio. Sounds hick, right? Nope. It was a well-to-do community outside Columbus with some of the most amazing families with some of the smartest and most beautiful girls on the planet.

Now what? I know nothing about pageants! Zip! Zero! Nada!

I was referred to Mr. Jim Outhouse. He was a lovely man who helped girls prepare for the pageant he so loved. He showed me videos of previous winners. The one that struck me was Suellen Cochran, Miss Ohio 1985, walking down the runway in her glistening white gown. She didn't walk; she floated with grace and ease. She was stunning and beautiful in her blonde eighties anchor-lady helmet hairdo. I would walk like that, I thought. Float. And so I did. (And I still do.)

He went into his "pageant closet." And he found a royal-blue number that kind of looked like a grandma gown, and he found a white polyester one-shoulder gown with silver and white sequins that looked like a rag up close but magical under stage lights. That would be my talent gown.

He attached a giant white-and-silver lily that was half the size of my head to the one shoulder. Add to that a big flower on the side of my overpermed hair, and voila! Off I went to compete. That night I got crowned Miss Pickerington in that royal-blue grandma gown and have photos to prove it.

So I won my first pageant ever and went to Miss Ohio that year, where I made the top ten.

The next year I would be Miss Canton, home of the Football Hall of Fame. Enter a new dress designer, Geri Baehr, who specialized in drag queens and pageantry of all kinds (shocking, I know). I chose the worst light-pink satin gown from a bridal magazine, and he made it for me. He also made a killer red beaded number for my talent performance, which I still treasure.

The pale-pink gown made its debut on the Miss Ohio Preliminary stage, to the horror of the judges. It hung on me like a garbage bag. I heard later that the judge's chair told them to ignore the dress. Miss Ohio gets a custom dress as part of her winnings. The judge's chair then sent back a messenger to tell me that I needed to wear anything but that dress for the final night. I had nothing else. But I did have that white one-shoulder hand-me-down.

So, off with the giant flower and on with a white feather boa. Hindsight would have been helpful here. But it was the eighties.

I was crowned Miss Ohio 1988 in that hand-me-down polyester gown, standing next to stunning $5,000 custom gowns.

CHAPTER 3
Evening Gown

You know the drill. Barbie clones parade around in glittery gowns, boobs on a platter, insanely high-heeled shoes, down a thirty-step lighted staircase, hitting their mark—and walk and turn and pose. I can personally tell you how painful that is. It takes discipline or insanity to deal with major foot pain, profuse sweating, loss of feeling in your jaws from smiling, and facial twitching while you're sucking in your tummy and praying that you don't trip and fall flat on your face or simply pass out from sucking everything in, and not eating or breathing. And the million-dollar answer to the secret question is...

In the pageant's defense, evening gowns are not just for pageants. They do come up in real life at proms, black-tie events, fundraisers, weddings, inaugural balls, red carpets, and so on. They appear as the ultimate celebration attire for our most-prized life honors and events. This is not the fault of the pageant. Pageantry has been around for centuries. Think of royalty and affluence and James Bond movies. The insanely hot and handsome man in formal wear has women falling at his feet in their couture evening gowns. And certainly, his Achilles' heel is gorgeous, powerful, lethal, highly intelligent women in said evening gowns. Formal wear is a huge part of our culture.

For those competing in the pageant that is real life, evening gown competition is about personal style. And it isn't just about dressing up for formal events. Your personal day-to-day style is one of the gifts you bring to the table. And let me be clear: the phrase "personal style" doesn't mean being dressed to the nines every day. It's the personal choice you make in how you want to present yourself to the world. **And we all have style—stating that you don't have a personal style that you stick to...well, I hate to tell you, but that's a personal style choice in and of itself. And what's more, it's a viable one.**

I'm a T-shirt, jeans, and flip-flops kind of gal—that's my personal style choice on a daily basis, and I will not apologize for it!

Don't like what is in style right now? Great! Thrift store shopping can be like a treasure hunt for vintage finds. Bonus: it's great girl time.

And what is more, it's about the confidence to make an entrance, work a room, deliver your thirty-second elevator pitch, and walk out with the funding for your life-saving research, rocket ship, or presidential campaign.

Moms! It all starts when our daughters are born into this world with all of who they are. Yes, they are influenced by their surroundings (nurture). But we all have a true nature that cannot be denied. And if it is, there is hell to pay, and nobody wants that!

Maybe you or your daughter would choose a sleek tuxedo instead of a gown.

I can tell you that my daughter would totally go for that! But it depends on the event and how she feels that day. I can't put her in a box, nor would I try. She loves seeing me in evening gowns for either a black-tie affair or when I am performing with a big band. She goes crazy for shiny bling things. And as much of a tomboy as she appears, she told me she wants to wear a princess gown for her wedding someday. What? Yep, turns out those big gowns are "practical" because you can move your legs around, and some even have pockets. Can't put that practical girl of mine in a box. What fun would that be anyway?

So how do we gear up for this part of life? ***As women showing up in this world and modeling behavior for our daughters, we must know who we are and embrace and love our own style, whatever that means.*** And we have to pay attention. Our daughters give us cues as to what they are attracted to. For instance, when my daughter was a baby, she would get frustrated in a dress. So for a while, she was strictly a pants girl. Happy girl = happy mom. Done and done.

I would discover that the combination of her personality and her clothing preferences said so much about who she was and is. Not too long ago, when discussing her decision to cut off her gorgeous long hair, she told me, "Mom, having long hair and having to spend time styling it is just not practical." Turns out she hated her long hair her whole life. It was too hot, and she simply was not interested in giving up her reading, drawing, and writing time to style it. She was also being typecast as the pretty, vapid longhaired girl at auditions during her acting phase. That totally sucked. But guess what? Her short hair with her bone structure makes her look even more gorgeous and feminine. Who knew? (She did.)

> *You don't have to be a fashionista to own your personal style. You don't need to drop a fortune at Saks, read Vogue regularly, or keep up with every trend. Being yourself is the best form of personal style.*

I was definitely a tomboy when I was younger. But I also loved wearing dresses and heels. So I can truly appreciate and relate to my daughter and any girl who enjoys having it all. Don't put us in a box, and God help us when we have that moment when we want our daughters to be a younger version of us. It happens. Just saying. Slippery slopes and fine lines loom large. Watch your step! Your daughter is not you, and vice versa.

What's in my closet? Mostly black, and I own a collection of miniskirts and dresses. I also have evening gowns and sexy cocktail dresses because I need them for events and singing performances. And I have workout clothes. What I struggle with is "mom clothes," which is an ongoing source of entertainment in my house. And that brings me to a few hard-and-fast rules regarding clothing choices.

Time and Place. I keep a few casual and modest items in my closet for school events. I also have dresses that are appropriate for church or funerals. I have taught my daughter about having respect for the occasion. So even though she only wears jeans and T-shirts, I make sure she has a couple of dresses and dress slacks that meet her approval in her closet when she needs them.

> *There is a time and place for everything, and that includes fashion. Your boobs, butt, and junk. Trust me: no one needs to see it while picking up a coffee or getting groceries.*

Another nonnegotiable rule is that you can show cleavage or legs but not both at the same time. I personally don't feel comfortable baring my chest and usually choose the showing-my-legs option. My daughter is very modest and doesn't feel comfortable baring anything. This rule requires a TMI check before leaving the house.

Before I go to an event, I always get her stamp of approval. It's a girlfriend thing we do. I let her help me pick out my dress, shoes, and jewelry and always do a check for appropriateness for the occasion. And we check for proper fit, any holes or rips, zippers, and buttons. There is nothing more embarrassing than going out in public with a wardrobe malfunction. But when I have had any issues, another woman always has my back. That's what we do. It's part of the sisterhood.

My daughter attends a private prep school and wears a uniform. Many girls don't like wearing them, but I feel that it is an honor and a privilege to be there. Wearing that uniform is a part of that. It keeps the students on the same playing field and not distracted by fashion. The students are able to focus on learning and developing as human beings. I love dropping her off and seeing how professional she looks. She loves looking professional too. And we don't have any drama about what she is going to wear—which, if you have a teenage girl, you know exactly the drama I speak of.

> *We don't always understand or like what our daughters wear. My only battle is time and place...or boobs, butt, and junk. Pick your battles wisely. You're welcome.*

Everyone has a personal style. It's not superficial. It's our most obvious daily expression of who we are. The possibilities are endless. If you live in a diverse place like Los Angeles, life is a daily parade of color, style, and culture. This brings me to another hard-and-fast rule regarding judging what other people are wearing.

When my daughter was three, she went through the pink-and-purple phase. For her it only lasted a couple of years. Then she hated pink and purple and would harshly judge other girls who were wearing those colors or girls obsessed with princess attire. We talked about honoring and celebrating people's fashion choices even if they aren't something we would choose for ourselves. I would see someone wearing bright colors or bold patterns and comment how gorgeous they looked. It makes me happy to see someone else wearing colors and styles that don't look good on me but look amazing on them.

This nonjudgement rule applies to pink, purple, tiaras, fluff, poof, and any other manner of fashion.

It takes courage to own your style. So let's have a little less judgement about our daughters' personal expression choices and more

> *Just because it's not your thing doesn't mean someone else can't rock it out. Enjoy the fashion show that is life!*

compassion for their journey to self-discovery. That acceptance will fuel their confidence to express themselves, as well as accept and honor the expression of others.

Pay attention. Be kind. Be yourself. We all shine much brighter and more beautifully when we do.

No crown required.

Flashback

Miss America Talent Competition

My singing talent was the reason I decided to compete. This part of the competition should have been a no-brainer. This was to be my time to really shine. Because I didn't just sing; I touched people with a message. My talent wasn't about me. It was about inspiring people. At twenty-one years of age, I already knew that.

Performing at the state pageant was done to the accompaniment of previously recorded music. But the Miss America Pageant upped the ante once again. You had the option of singing with a live orchestra. As a seasoned entertainer, who wouldn't go for that? This would be a lesson in trusting your own people and understanding the gravity of a situation.

Less than a month before Atlantic City, I was given a cassette tape of an orchestra arrangement of my song. I don't remember much about rehearsing with it. I only remember that it didn't sound quite right and thinking I would somehow pull it off when I got there.

I got one shot at rehearsal before the competition. And the orchestra was reading my chart for the first time. So it was the first time for all of us. I didn't even recognize my own song. I still thought I could pull it off. That night during the competition, I was trying to slow the orchestra down, but the conductor interpreted my arm waving as a speed-up signal. I was in full panic mode the whole time. I wasn't connecting with the audience, and I was miserable.

One of my best friends, Dana P. Rowe, had done my original recorded arrangement. We spent years performing together in clubs and musical theatre. He has since become a successful and beloved Broadway show composer and arts mentor. The pageant people brought in another arranger, and I didn't have the consciousness or the confidence to insist on my brilliantly talented best friend for the job. I would have recognized his arrangement. And he was "my people." We made magic together.

I did not win talent that night and did not get to perform on national television. Although I did end up with a non-finalist talent award, my self-esteem took a big hit that night. It would be one of many hits that would eventually take a toll.

The wisdom I garnered from that experience has proven to be the most valuable. Know your amazing people, hold them close, and take them with you.

CHAPTER 4
Talent

The Miss America Pageant talent competition conjures visions of fire-baton twirling, classical pianists who only know one song, and painful moments of mediocre singers and dancers. There was once even a young woman who packed a suitcase on stage. And in 2014, Miss New York was crowned after sitting on the stage floor banging on a red cup. That pretty much beats the suitcase girl hands down.

Besides endless jokes about world peace, it is the talent competition that incites the most criticism. Unlike some other pageants that are primarily focused on beauty and swimsuit, the Miss America Pageant ups the ante by requiring its competitors to showcase performance art.

It's rare to find a smart, savvy young girl with a perfect physique, a platform to save the world, public speaking skills, and professional-level performance art prowess. Just writing that list of qualifications is daunting. And the expectations of the talent portion of the competition have increased with the saturation of singing and dancing competitions designed to elevate the winners to idol status.

Our culture is inundated with fame or being famous for performance art talents. This fame is valued over everything else. Most people think of only music and art as talent. And there are studies that prove that having and expressing fine art in our lives elevates our brains and our being. While I believe that is true, I don't believe that someone who doesn't have those gifts isn't talented.

Why is talent an important tool in our toolbox for life? And what is talent? This is a tricky subject and one I find incredibly personal.

I was raised dancing, playing the piano, and singing since early childhood. The singing thing was so strong in me that I knew that it would be my life's work (the songwriting came much later and the book-writing thing even later), so for me this was a no-brainer. I had been a performer my whole life. It was the main reason I was competing in the pageant.

Be adventurous! Always. Try new things, and live your life to the fullest.

I wanted to share my love for singing and playing the piano with my daughter. Some families are so musical! It was a brief dream I would have to let go of. She tried it and had the talent, but it wasn't her thing. Of course, I was disappointed at first, but her happiness meant more to me. ***So if you are a parent who regrets not sticking with the piano, don't make your kids do it for you. Treat yourself to some lessons.***

I was once told by my daughter's pre-K teacher,

Miss Tina, that you can pretty much tell what children will do when they grow up by just watching them interact with one another and their environment. They are born with likes and dislikes and certain skills or gifts. They develop through nature and nurture: the tendencies they are born with and the influences of their environment. Her insight really made me think. And it made me pay attention.

As I started to pay more attention to our unique daughter, her gifts and passions were revealing themselves all the time.

Turns out since she was a baby, she was staring at books instead of sticking her finger in a light socket (which might have indicated more of a science interest). And I do mean for hours at a time. Her grandma sent boxes of books she found at yard sales. Nightly bedtime stories read out loud by a dramatic mom fueled her gift for storytelling and an ear for voices and accents. Despite her dad being a gifted designer, a friend at school who was good at art would be the first influence to spark her massive passion for drawing. Her specialty? Cartoons, graphic novels, animation, and writing. And later, as we placed her in more stimulating environments with good energy, she would keep discovering other fun activities that brought her great joy.

It is essential to honor all kinds of gifts and talents, even if they are not art or music. Math, science, sewing, the healing arts, writing, photography, filmmaking, acting, sports, cooking, dancing, fashion, gardening. Banking and accounting even. The list is endless. The point is to fill your life with the things you love to do. Some may be your career and some may be your hobbies, and one may be your passion.

Pay attention. If your child is obsessed with something and hates to go to lessons, look closer. Now mind you, no kid wants to practice. But some teachers may not click with you or your daughter. Can you remember a favorite teacher who made you love a subject? This is the same thing. And it is especially important because whatever creative endeavor you are engaging in is supposed to be fun.

> *Don't stay with something because you think you have to, or force your daughter to, either. If it's not for you, leave it behind, and explore the new options ahead of you.*

I had been taking voice lessons since I was ten. When I was in high school, I went to a new teacher. She was a mezzo soprano with a thick, heavy voice. I was a coloratura soprano, which is a lighter and much higher voice. (This was before my gift of my alto belt voice came to my attention.) She basically told me that I did not have "the voice," which I knew was not true. It just wasn't like hers. My mom remembers me marching out to the car in tears and saying that I wouldn't be going back. And I did not go back.

Be careful when looking for teachers. Follow your gut. If it feels icky, it is icky. And trust your daughter's feelings too. Choose your daughter's trainer, coach, or sensei wisely.

A great friend, Miss Ohio 1990, Kristin Huffman,

has a beautiful operatic voice. She recently told me that the Miss Ohio directors tried to get her to sing something pop at Miss America. I couldn't believe it, knowing her talent. They said that a pop singer was what they thought the pageant was going for. She was smart and confident enough to stick with her forte, which landed her in the top five at Miss America and eventually a Broadway show.

Kristin's story inspired me. Confidence. It reminded me to keep trusting in who I am. A lesson I keep needing to learn. I now only surround myself with people who are in love with my talent and support me on my chosen path. That wisdom is a gift for me and my daughter.

> *Everyone has talents. Don't forget to take the time to find out what yours are. Your spirit will thank you.*

You can't force true talent. True talent unfolds on its own. Finding your true talent is easy. It is the thing you can't stop doing. For amazing musicians, it's the thing that makes you lock yourself in your room and work away until you drop. And then you do it some more. You can't make that happen for your child. But pay attention. There is something your child loves to do that will enrich her life and yours. You may have to think about limiting TV and gaming time, or you may never know her gift, and neither will she.

Another important concept I remind my daughter of is to block out the naysayers when it comes to pursuing her talents. The saboteurs of the world will say there is way too much competition for you to succeed, implying that you won't be a person who breaks through. No matter how many people are in your field or artistic discipline, there is only one you. ***Believe that your passions were born in you for a reason, and surround yourself with people who believe that too.***

> *Even if you have natural talent, you still have to hone your craft. Natural talent alone isn't going to get you there (unless you are a demigod).*

Expressing our talents is a critical part of being in full expression and making the most of our human experience. Allow yourself to discover and express your gifts, and you will inspire your daughter to do the same.

The long journey of talent mastery requires compassion in yourself for the process. Every milestone instills confidence. All it takes is the courage to begin.

No crown required.

Flashback

Interview, Atlantic City Hotel

I entered the large, shiny, stark-white marble hallway that led to an unfamiliar conference room. It was time. I found my place in the long line of waiting contestants. We all knew this was where the pageant was won—what clinched the deal. We would each have seven minutes to see if the odds were in our favor for a "love connection" with five very savvy people whose heads would be spinning at the task they were charged to do.

I was numb. Numb so I wouldn't feel the terror I was trying hard to conceal. This didn't feel like the magical times before, when I was cracking jokes in the holding area to lighten the mood and make my fellow contestant friends laugh. Being funny was my thing. It broke the ice for everyone. Mostly me. It gave me access to my best self. It is one of my gifts, my secret weapon, but not that day.

"Clumsy Miss Ohio trips out of her shoe" the newspaper coverage read. Yes, that would be shared with the whole country. It was the event where we all got introduced in a hotel ballroom with a makeshift runway with cracks in between, where my stiletto heel got lodged. I made it funny at the time.

I began to realize that I had something deeper going on that would sabotage my chances. I was wearing a long white pleated silk skirt and matching blouse with silver beading. With my blonde hair in that white hall, I blended in with the surrounding walls and floor. My parade gown was white, my bathing suit was white, and my evening gown was white. Pure as the driven snow. Miss America, your ideal!

There was a part of me that felt as if I got my virginity back when I was crowned. I wanted to be that wholesome, perfect, beautiful girl whom people looked to for inspiration. But I felt like a fraud. I felt dirty and ashamed of certain aspects of my life and was afraid they would find out that I wasn't good enough to be their role model.

I did not feel funny, colorful, confident, or smart. I was scared.

And then it happened. I got the dreaded question about premarital sex. I can't remember if they asked me if I had it or how I felt about it. But I felt sick and faint, and the rest was a blur. No magic. No funny. No connection.

Not my panel of judges. Not my day.

CHAPTER 5

Interview

The pageant is won or lost in the interview. And it's the only thing that isn't shown to the public. So while the television and live audiences are making their choices based on all outer visual criteria, each judge pretty much knows going into the final night who is their winner. She's the one who "had them at hello" in the interview.

This is where fate and luck come into play. Because there are five different judges with different life experiences, opinions, interests, degrees of awareness, and taste, any of the girls who make it to this national level have a legitimate shot.

When I competed, there was a seven-minute interview with five judges. You received their bios ahead of time, so you could get plenty nervous about trying to impress these usually much older, wiser, more worldly, and often famous people. And they got to look at a one-sheet bio that you had filled out so they could decide at first glance what they wanted to know more about. You had better be able to explain yourself. It sounds easy. But it is not for a very young woman—unless you have really taken the time to go within and know yourself. And you must practice explaining yourself in a clear, pleasant, and concise manner so that when those pesky nerves hit—and they will with a vengeance—you will handle it like a pro. Your competition certainly will.

What do you stand for? You must declare a "platform." Save the oceans, feed the hungry, stop human trafficking? Maybe. Your platform should be something relevant and timely. A cause for which you have done some major work or invested time and effort toward saving whatever and whoever you are saving! It has to be something people really care about or can learn to care about more because of you.

> *Go! Do things. Read things. Read, read, read. Learn about the world around you. I promise you will thank yourself one day.*

And yes, world peace is too general a topic.

Mostly, your platform must be something you are passionate about. The rest, as stated above, is luck and timing. ***You can't fake what you care about, and you shouldn't. Be authentic, or people will not connect with you at all. This is true about life in general.***

The rest of the questions are unknown to you. The judges can ask you anything they want! It can be world geography, politics, war, movies, or literature. They can ask you to name your congresswoman and who sits on the Supreme Court. Current events and world issues are all fair game. Women's rights, abortion, gun control, religion. The possibilities made my head spin. And if you are going to win, you are going to have to get your head in the game and put on your best dog-and-pony show!

Oh yes, that is right. I said dog-and-pony show! Are you smart, funny, charming, and clever? Are you lovable? Are you comfortable answering questions you don't know the answers to? What about those inappropriate questions? Can you redirect when they get on a tangent that isn't in your expertise? Are you quick witted and press savvy? Do you put everyone at ease? Is your voice calm and mature? Do you have charisma? Can we feel the love?

> *Talking about what you feel and stand for on a regular basis is great practice for an interview. Take the time to write down every question that could come up. Research the issues at hand, and search your own heart for how you truly feel about them. Write it all down. That list of questions will continue to grow. Then, practice by having someone ask you those questions. We can do that for our daughters. Take it a step further, and find other trusted friends to mock interview her.*

How well do you know yourself? How well do you know the world? What are you doing to make the world a better place? People who think that the contestants who make it to that Miss America stage are simply vapid beauty queens (who can't pass by a mirror without looking) would be amazed at the wisdom and poise of these remarkable women.

Pageant contestants are vying for the job of representing the Miss America program for a whole year. That job is meant to essentially be a spokesperson for women in America. She won't wear a swimsuit all year, and rarely will she perform her talent. She will attend tons of functions, make TV appearances, and be expected to give compelling speeches. She will be scrutinized every minute of the year she wears that crown.

I have said this before, but it bears repeating. Some of the most exceptional women I have known are women I met in that two years of my involvement with the Miss America Pageant. I have also met some seriously clueless girls and their stage moms. The latter don't usually get that far.

Being prepared for this kind of interview doesn't just come in handy for winning a pageant. These young women will eventually interview for their dream job, and because they have mastered this skill, they will probably get it.

I want my daughter to be the one who "has them at hello." And no, I can't ever see her being in a pageant. She abhors the idea, and I get it.

This all starts when they are little. If you get into the habit of talking about a wide variety of things on a regular basis, it will be her normal. And when it is appropriate, begin to talk about more serious issues going on in her world and the world at large.

I was always close to my mom and could talk

Know the issues. They aren't just issues. The issues relate to the human condition, and it matters. Vote. Have the conversation. Even if your kids' opinions align with yours, they should understand why.

to her about anything. And I did. My dad was always the kind of dad I could count on no matter what. He was always on call to come and pick me up any time of day or night, which he did on numerous occasions, no matter how far away I was or how many friends I had with me. My parents lived for their girls, family, and each other. They knew we each had gifts that could take us far, and they believed in us even when we couldn't believe in ourselves.

I got my heart for all people from my parents. As empty nesters, they finally had time to be of service to their community. I am inspired by them every single day.

The thing we didn't talk about was how to fail. The message was this: if you can't do something right, don't do it at all. I was afraid to fail and obsessed with perfection. I would come to understand that anything we eventually master must have been preceded by a lot of mistakes—by failure.

And most likely we will be mediocre or terrible at it at first. Success has more to do with passion and perseverance.

Even though I won the first pageant I entered at age nineteen, I found out that I had a long way to go to master the interview. One of the judges from the first pageant was Geri Zettler. She and her husband, Bob, were the directors of the Miss Ohio Pageant. She gave me her phone number after and told me to call her if I wanted feedback.

I will never forget that phone call. I was sitting on the living room floor of my campus apartment on beige carpeting, nervous and excited about what she might say to me. She began by telling me that my talent and swimsuit were both amazing. Then she said, "Your hair looks like a fried mess. But that is fixable." That eighties perm was horrifying for sure. Then she said, "Your evening gown looks like something a grandma would wear." Another fixable thing. "In your interview, you came across as cocky." The other fixable items stung a little, but this one was like a gut punch. I was super confident about competing, especially because of the talent part, but the interview part was all new to me.

> Listen. Be open, and consider both sides of every argument.

Then she ended our brief conversation by saying, "I know you are going to be Miss Ohio one day." That conversation marked the beginning of a journey of cracking the code of how to do just that, which involved my first big lesson in humility. ***It would be the embracing of humility that turned my cockiness into confidence and critique into self-improvement.***

I hit a home run in my interview to win the Miss Ohio Pageant and then went on to have a crisis of confidence at Miss America. Even if we think we've mastered this interview thing, we will have good and bad experiences. It's all a part of the ups and downs of life. The bigger the prize, the greater the pressure. ***We grow into wisdom as we continue to know ourselves better and are brave enough to show up for each challenge.***

It would take a personal journey starting in my late twenties to fully understand what the missing pieces of my life-skills puzzle were. I made my parents a part of that journey. My current husband played a huge role. And now my daughter is the beneficiary of all that wisdom and love.

Do we have to be smarter than everyone to win?

I am surrounded by very intelligent people. My daughter is one of them. Something we talk about often is that everyone is smart in different ways. Some people are street smart, and some have advanced degrees. And while intellectual intelligence is a trait I admire, I value emotional intelligence far more. When we find ourselves stuck in our heads, I always say, "Get out of your head, and shift into your heart space." Love is there. Charisma is there. Fun is there. Peace is there.

> *Know yourself, but don't label yourself. You're supercool, but don't get stuck defining yourself in such a way that you can't learn and grow every day.*

I know I'm smart, but I don't need to be the smartest person in the room. There are people who feel the need to be just that. And they are no fun to be around. There is freedom in giving up the need to know all the answers or know more than someone else. And there is fun in being surrounded by people who know stuff we don't know.

My daughter attends a school with some of the smartest and brightest young women in the country. The competition is fierce. Egos and academic pressure

> *You are not defined by your personality test, gender identification, or IQ. Never let anyone else tell you otherwise.*

loom large. Surviving and thriving are the end game.

She knows she is not in competition with any of them. She focuses on being and doing her best. My reminder to her is "Stay in your own lane." She realizes that sometimes she needs to reach out for help, and sometimes her classmates will need to reach out. It's part of the sisterhood.

Most important is the "know yourself" piece of this puzzle. And just as I have stated in the previous chapters about listening to your daughter, remember that she truly does know who she is and what she cares about. Take the time to find out without always projecting on her what is important to you or what you think should be important. That's harder than it sounds. I have at times failed on that one for sure.

Fear of public speaking is well known as one of the scariest things for most of the population. Whether that is true or not, know that it takes time to develop this skill.

My daughter gets nervous and frustrated about expressing herself in a speech or a meeting with a teacher. She is an introvert. She's also confessed to me that she worries about what other people think. I know how she feels. When I was sixteen, I wasn't the speaker I am now. I tell her, "It took me a lifetime to get to this place, and you are way ahead of me! Take a deep breath, and keep showing up. Even the best speakers aren't perfect. Making mistakes can be funny if you have a good sense of humor." I trust that will come with time, since I am her mom. But I know it's hard for my very serious daughter to trust that it will come to pass. Sometimes I get frustrated because I know how funny she is with me, and I want the world to see her as I do. That is when I need to take a deep breath and just be fully present and accept where she is now. And that is a pretty amazing place. I tell her that too.

We live and learn. We learn to listen to our daughters because when we do, they open up and begin to share and truly know themselves and love themselves for who they are.

That leads to them sharing their wisdom, wit, and charm with the world in wonderful ways. Who doesn't want that? This is that "inner beauty" part. It is the true beauty we all aspire to.

> *I can never say this enough: Be curious! Never stop learning new things. Have conversations about anything and everything!*

And don't we all need to find a cause that speaks to our heart and give back in some way? This is the compassion piece of the puzzle. Getting out of our heads and living in our heart space is essential. Happiness lives there.

Self-awareness gives us confidence to connect in high-pressure situations and the courage to share our vision with the world.

No crown required.

Flashback

Ohio Stadium Halftime Show

I couldn't wrap my head around the news. The day I left for Atlantic City, there was an Ohio State University football game. Someone had pulled some surprising strings to give me the best send-off ever. I get chills thinking about it because as a huge fan of "The Best Damn Band In The Land," I was going to get the gift of a lifetime.

When I was a student at The Ohio State University, I used to go to their skull sessions before the game to hear them warm up. Then, at halftime, The Ohio State University Marching Band would make their entrance through the tunnel into the stadium in such a dramatic way to a crazed crowd of ninety thousand screaming students, fans, rivals, and alumni. Pure magic. They would always surprise and delight the masses with brilliant formations, and their sound was so tight and can only be described as "perfection."

The band had just completed the script Ohio formation. The announcer introduced "our very own Miss Ohio." I was escorted, in my scarlet business suit, with huge eighties hair and shoulder pads, onto the field, where I led the stadium in singing our beloved alma mater.

I had never been on the field before, and looking up at the sea of scarlet and gray, I had yet another moment on this journey of knowing this wasn't about me. I was going to represent my state and my school, and I had thousands of people cheering me on. I was their Miss Ohio, and I wanted to make them proud.

That day I was a girl who was heading to the "big show" on a private plane after what would be one of the most humbling experiences in my life.

CHAPTER 6
The Bad and the Ugly

Competing in a pageant can be as brutal as any other major competition you will face in your life. There are politics and bullying, judgement and shaming.

At the age when you may compete, you aren't fully able to process it all. You're not your wisest and best self yet. There are things that happen that are not so pretty.

Gowns were ruined. Shoes disappeared. "You're wearing that?" One even had her torso duct taped. This was before Spanx was a thing. And some girls were so in their zone that they couldn't crack a smile backstage. Me? I spent most of the time making everyone laugh. And I witnessed firsthand the pressures that stage parents put on their daughters to validate their lineage. It's a hot mess.

Backstage you'll find contestants pulling swimsuit bottoms up their crack so someone can spray sport stick on their butt cheeks so the swimsuit won't ride up when the girls walk out on stage. Vaseline, I found, didn't work to ease the smiling thing. It just gets your teeth red from lipstick. I had to put cotton in my belly button so you couldn't see the dent through my swimsuit.

There were moments that left me dumbfounded, such as the evaluation of my ugly face. When talking with another Miss Ohio, I learned they had recommended that she get a nose job.

Then there was that time I was sent to the home of someone who was supposed to prepare me for Miss America. The people weren't around when I arrived. But they did have a very handsome and charismatic eighteen-year-old son who spent time with me. He made screwdrivers, and we ended up making out in their den only to be busted by his mother. I was shamed, and they pretty much didn't talk to me after that. That is some serious training right there.

And there was that time after I left the Ohio Stadium from my amazing send-off and hopped in the private plane, only to learn they had left my luggage on the tarmac. Glad I liked my arrival outfit. All the other contestants were changing into their "check-in" outfits. I think I needed a cocktail then too. Truth? My check-in outfit was ugly. Hindsight says that the universe was trying to pull some strings for me after all.

And then there is that parade of the states in Corvette convertibles down the famous Atlantic City Boardwalk. "Show us your shoes!" the crowd would shout at each one. I was not fully prepped coming into that parade about the importance and sophistication of the shoe tradition. The contestants had elaborate, state-inspired, blinged-out artistic creations of Manhattan skylines and I don't know what all. Me? Someone made me a brown furry ball of a slipper that was a buckeye.

Only Ohio State fans would know it as our beloved mascot, which is a poisonous nut. As sweet as it was, no one knew what it was. And I got shouts about it, including "Is that poop?" Yes! I am wearing stuffed poop! Really?

The Miss Ohio who preceded me hit the national papers with the infamous quote "I was robbed!" after she didn't make top ten at the Miss America Pageant. They called her "Ohio's finest whine." She also told reporters that the state troopers would let her get away with speeding. Not sure of any of the other details of her "reign." I can only imagine. The aftermath was brutal, and the state pageant would have a hard time getting sponsors on board. I was the only Miss Ohio who didn't get a car to drive for the year. That was fine. I had a sexy red Mustang I loved, and you can bet those state troopers were gunning for me.

And in fact I did get pulled over in a small town, and when the officer asked my profession, I told him I was Miss Ohio. He didn't bat an eye or inquire about my answer and kept writing the ticket, handed it to me, and walked back to his cruiser. When I looked at the ticket, it said, in the space for employment, "Sohio." Big belly laugh for me and a humbling moment of "Who cares?" He thought I worked for the gas station chain.

So I had an ugly gown, an ugly face, and questionable decision-making regarding handsome boys and alcohol. I had ugly pictures and bad timing. I was clumsy and insecure and wore poop.

I learned much later about the saying "It's all material." Even then I knew it was funny. How boring would life be if everything were easy and perfect? And yes, I've got more secrets in the vault, the layers of which come and go. Best kept marinating for now.

CHAPTER 7
The Good

I have been honest about my criticism that the Miss America Pageant does not truly represent all women in America. And now I need to write a love letter about the good that came from it all.

It all started with my voice professor, who proved to be my biggest fan and gave me that nudge to face a challenge that would change my life for good. It makes me think how we all have a chance to whisper "Go get 'em" and "I believe in you" and "You're amazing!" in someone's ear. And how it matters more than you think. If you are reading this and you don't have someone whispering these messages in your ear, you are with the wrong people. Consider your exit plan ASAP. And consider that we as moms get to do the whispering, and make sure the people in your daughter's circle are too.

What people who aren't involved in the Miss America Pageant don't know about is the driving force behind it all. It's the volunteers who celebrate, support, mentor, and believe in our girls. Yes, our girls. It really does take a village. From the house moms to the chaperones to the pageant directors, sponsors, hometowns, and people who put on the shows—they all give their time, talent, and treasure straight from their hearts for the singular cause of empowering young women to be their best selves. Yes, there are some bad apples. But you'll find that in life too. I've had some pretty special heart-centered people in my corner whom I still consider family. Too many names to mention.

The outpouring of support from friends and family touched my heart deeply. Cards, notes, and gifts all in scrapbooks my mom recently sent to me. I couldn't believe how many.

The friendship of Dana Rowe. Those magical music arrangements he gifted me and that over-the-top celebration party. To this day he remains my biggest fan, close friend, and mentor.

It was a treat to perform with another BFF, Andy Haines, renowned show choir choreographer. Andy looked better in my swimsuit than I did. There is a photo of that somewhere. I wish I had known that he could be backstage with me in Atlantic City as my makeup and hair guy. I found out later how people bend the rules. In hindsight, I'm not sure the pageant could have handled both Andy and me backstage at the same time.

The first year of competing and only making top ten in my state pageant, I was devastated. I was not a good loser and was embarrassingly crying my eyes out. Backstage we were all packing up our things, and Sarah Ann Evans came up to me to give me a hug. "We'll get 'em next year," she said. I told her I wouldn't be back. I'll never forget that moment. That next year I did come back, and I became Miss Ohio. The year after that, I crowned Sarah.

It didn't dawn on me until recently that I'd become a member of a very small, very special sorority. I was never homecoming or prom queen. I was rejected by college sororities. I finally found my tribe of women.

Who can say they have been in practically every nook and cranny of the State of Ohio? Miss Ohio can. Who has keys to several cities in Ohio? Miss Ohio does. There were countless parades, festivals, pageants, dinners, and celebrations of culture, cuisine, and beauty. Every family I met and every young woman I encouraged along that trek started to change me. I went from a performer who only thought of the stage to a young woman who couldn't stop thinking about the people and how I could inspire and elevate their human experience by connecting with them and honoring them. More good. It made me rethink what I wanted to do with my life.

It was three months from the state pageant in June to the national pageant in September. My mom, a sixth-grade teacher, had summers off. We made memories that we still laugh about all the time. Turns out I'm a pretty good marksman in heels. We learned that at the Annie Oakley festival. And those endless mayoral luncheons inspired the name of our summer tour, the Chicken Salad Circuit. Good thing we liked chicken salad. I taught my mom to push her food around her plate so it looked like she ate something—important when you've just had a huge breakfast and are heading to another dinner party. We learned a new term for attire, country club casual. Sounds easy, right? But it meant different things everywhere we went. We were never dressed appropriately and probably still couldn't crack that code. I trained my mom to mingle with people. She was painfully shy and remembers me giving her the evil eye from across the table or room. That was her not-so-subtle cue to smile and chat. Turns out she was quite the social butterfly and still is. She loves people. So many more mom-and-me stories to tell, but the end game was priceless memories made laughing and exploring our great state. I couldn't have done it all without her and will always feel grateful that I didn't have to.

I was always close to my mom. We were best friends, and this was just the icing on the cake. Sharing that experience was a gift for us both. Many years later I would plan the birth of my baby girl around her summer schedule. All that goodness I shared with my mom, I couldn't wait to share with my daughter.

And now I get to be that close to my daughter. We are indeed best friends and have already had quite the adventures together and way more inside jokes than anyone within earshot of us can possibly stand.

The stuff that crashed and burned, the bad and the ugly and the people who disappointed, were all part of the journey. And your daughter will have all of that too.

How amazing it feels to help our daughters navigate from a place of life experience. To know that every failure or disappointment is just a small blip of material to giggle over later when their

moment to shine finally comes. And it will come—not just once, but so many times. There will be so many magical moments that it is impossible to fathom.

Whisper that in her ear.

Flashback

Being Crowned Miss Ohio

They called my name! Crown...sash...roses...and walk...runway...lights. Uncontrollably crying and shaking, I didn't know it would affect me that way. I had always made fun of the crying winner. And now she was me. Hell, I had always made fun of the pageant in general, and now this.

They liked me! They really liked me! I was the underdog. I was the girl from a blue-collar family wearing the hand-me-down gown. The judges, friends, family, teachers, and my parents in that packed house of people whose daughters I competed with side by side were all standing, smiling, and clapping. I looked deep into each of their faces and was overwhelmed with love and gratitude.

It was the first moment I would realize fully that this wasn't about me. I felt humbled by the amazing young women I had competed with. Any other night, with any other panel of judges, any of those girls could have been standing where I was. I was in fierce company, and I knew it. Luck and timing. It was my turn. And it didn't seem real at all.

Backstage in an empty hallway, the pageant director, Bob Zettler, stood smiling. "We've been waiting for you."

CHAPTER 8
And Finally...

I didn't win, place, or show in Atlantic City that year. And as much as that broke my heart at the time, it wasn't my path. I would go on to pursue my music, writing, coaching, and many other life adventures, including being a mom.

Life isn't always fair or easy. But it is rich with choices, twists and turns, and unexpected miracles. Like having a daughter I never knew I even wanted. Until I did. And what an amazing gift she is.

It was having a daughter that led me back to my true essence. My purpose to share wisdom I "came in" with. My passion to tell stories that make people laugh and feel inspired. My gift to connect with the world through love and compassion. My obsession with seeing beauty all around me and in everyone I meet.

I know what I want for my daughter. I want her to have the tools I didn't have when faced with the obstacles, competition, and losses that life brings. I want her to crack the code.

I know that if I can help her embrace all these areas of competition from the start, she will be well on her way to having the confidence needed to go after her biggest and wildest dreams. And have a legitimate shot at realizing them.

And that brings me to the happiness part. ***We all want our daughters to be happy. We want to be happy. Happiness happens when we are living in our truth, in full expression of our gifts. Happiness is being healthy, grateful and giving back to make a difference in the world.***

The Miss America Pageant started out as a swimsuit beauty contest on the boardwalk of a town desperately needing to attract tourist dollars. Because of the amazing young women who braved that runway over the years, it has evolved into so much more. I'm sure they didn't see that one coming. And yes, they have a long way to go. I believe they will get there. After all, they are dealing with women—intelligent, heart-centered women of purpose who see it as a platform or vehicle to effect change and heal what is wounded in the world.

We are the self-realized healers, teachers, protectors, guardians, and fighters. We are the game changers raising new world leaders.

We are the sisterhood.

The concepts I have shared in this book are only the beginning of the wisdom and conversations I have shared with my daughter since she was born. I'm humbled and amazed by our relationship every day.

If you are resonating with what I have shared and are already implementing these tools in your life, you have already won.

Confidence, courage, and compassion.
No crown required.

CHAPTER 9
...Wrap It Up in a Bow!

GIVE HER SINCERE PROPS.

I always make it a point to tell my daughter often, "I wouldn't change a thing about you. I love the way your brain works. You are so much fun to be around. Your obsession with the things you love is inspiring. I miss you when I don't get enough time with you. I can't wait to see what happens next. You are so beautiful. I love how you light up like a Christmas tree when you are talking about something you love. How did I get to be so lucky?" Keep a running list! You are going to need more paper.

TALK ABOUT HER BEHIND HER BACK.

It started when she was little and I would be on the phone with my mom. Bragging about what she was up to, about how much I loved being her mom, and about how she was so smart and funny was a regular long-distance phone thing. Making sure she was within earshot of that every once in a while proved to be a good thing. On the other hand, make sure when you are venting about not-so-good stuff, she *isn't* within earshot. The best way to ruin your trust and friendship is her hearing you talk bad about her.

IX-NAY ON THE ITICISM-CRAY.

Criticism? You are her mom, not a critic. She knows how she is doing and what kind of progress she wants to make. I can't tell you how important this is. Leave it to her art teacher, her coach, or whoever is guiding her. I am simply in awe of anything she presents to me. Usually I ask her how she feels about it. Then I have to tell her I am amazed at her passion and how she just keeps getting better at everything she puts her mind to. In the interest of transparency, I have been the critic, and it feels icky to this day.

DISPLAYING A NOT-SO-GOOD TRAIT OR BEHAVIOR?

So many different times to use this one, but I love telling her how *I love* how neat she keeps her room. And I love that she loves being in a neat space. Even when it is a disaster area. Or, when she is struggling with kindness or patience, I tell her she is one of kindest people I know. And that her patience is epic, even when it doesn't feel that way. She gets to be human. And she gets to remember that even on a bad day, she gets to remember her true essence is good.

VENTING ABOUT SOMETHING WE HATE IS FUN!

Math. Let's just start there. Math can go to hell! I love to chime in on that one. She and I are creatives and love our math-loving friends, but seriously, we would rather use our brains for other things. Can't tell you how many times we have bonded over stuff we hate!

TCB, BABY!

She is actually very good at math and quantitative reasoning. I tell her to kick math's butt, knowing that soon—and very soon—she can kick it to the curb. Strangely, she started getting A's in math. That is just one bitter pill we love to rant about in fun and funny ways. Life is full of them. After math goes away, there will be something else to take its place. To win at this life thing, we have to take care of business!

RAISE THE BAR.

Pay close attention to her friendships. Start when she is little. I was able to help her identify mean girls and passive-aggressive types early on. She was very clueless about that, but now she has great radar. Toxic people don't last, which means toxic boyfriends won't either. SCORE!

Reality check: She will have to date that one boy with the leather jacket whom her dad will want to punch. I did. I can still smell the pheromones.

I APOLOGIZE. SINCERELY.

Apologize when you make a mistake. Being human is complicated.

Did you yell too loud? Overreact? I have. It comes from old programming. I am honest about my shortcomings, and I check myself. It is always about our own stuff. I ask for forgiveness. She always grants it, every time. My daughter is also a person who sometimes yells too loud, overreacts, and lashes out in fear or anger. And she knows I will grant forgiveness.

As parents, we strive to be the best we can be, but we are only human. Admitting mistakes and taking responsibility is key. When we are allowed to fail and make mistakes without fear of judgement and rejection, we can move on and raise a daughter who can do the same.

It's about having a relationship. For me it was never about having a "baby." When I did, it was because I wanted to have a lifelong relationship with a human. And an amazing human is what I got. Lucky me.

"I wouldn't change a thing about you."

ACKNOWLEDGMENTS

My husband Larry, my daughter Elizabeth

Mom and Dad

To our family, the Wyatts and the Johnsons, near and far, for all of these years of your love and support in person and in cards and letters of encouragement. I thank you.

Dana Rowe: Without your guidance I wouldn't have remembered that I know how to crack the code.

Andy Haines: for telling me thirty years ago I should write a book. Hold on to your hat!

Dr. Paul Hickfang: for whispering in my ear.

Tracy Balsz: Public Relations and dream-come-true-maker

Sandy Karp, SDK Design: Book Cover Design, Creative

Shawn Flint Blair: Photographer

Editors in peeps!

Carol Woodliff: Hand holder, Shaman, Cat Sitter, and Book Doula

Larry Wyatt, Elizabeth Wyatt, Andrea Randall, Scott Sigman, Melissa Gersh, Trisha Becker

Final Edit: Tracy Balsz

Trusted friends who braved to read my final draft and gave me feedback:

Laura Perry, Christina Chaparro, Kristin Schmidt, Kelly Lester, Heather Hubara, Karen Finnochio, Leslie Ann McCord, Jenefer Gee Combs, Elisa All Schmitz, Kathy Gardener Pinto, Betty Coss, Carolyn Chambers, Sally Dier, LM Jobson, Lana Santos, Barb Free, Gregg Jackson, Rebecca Chernack, Heather Frey, Meredith Schneider, Kerri Gruber, Lana Kantos, Kim Brendzal, Steven Oliveri, Beth Baumeister, and Kristin Showalter

More Believers, Inspirers, Heart Space Holders, and Cheerleaders:

Christina Chaparro, Carol Woodliff, Gayle Blickle-Reilich, Marcie May, Karen Busko, Holly Lyn Brown, Melanie Namesiv, Britt Michaelian, Kasi and Rob Peters, Susan Andres, Kerri Gruber, Chloe Gruber, Brianna Fawn, Lauren Johnson, Donna Gannon, Beverly Thompson-Warren, Mary Anne Layne, Rasheeda Azar, Zephryn Conte, Roxy Rocker, Cecil Thomas Jr., Michael Sechrest, Marina Rice-Bader, Sharon Bates, Katie McClain, Stephen Dimmick, Carla Renata, Kristin Huffman, Sarah Ann Evans-Tackett, Sheila Rossi, Jocelyn Good, Ami LeMaster, Ginger Matthews-Santulli, Sam Kriger, Marilyn Roth, Hal and Helen Thomas, Karen Timko, Judy Tsai, Julie Tutokey, Lisa Akey, Paul Ward, Deena Willis, Colleen Zallow, Dori Zuckerman, Sheila Boggess Young, Rebel Brown, Lance Rickman, Terry Landry, Tracy Kahaner, Nick Winslow, Jodi Persson, Jim Stoner, Ogun Holder, Erika Diamond, Marcia Papalas, Lyn Boyd-Judson, Michele Sinisgalli-Yulo, Lea Compton, Lori Moreno, Robin Reiter

The Ohio State University, OSU Alumni, and Buckeye Nation.

The Best Damn Band in the Land (The Ohio State University Marching Band).

Warren Western Reserve High School, Raider Nation.

The Miss Ohio Organization, The Miss America Pageant, and the Town of Mansfield, Ohio:

Especially my pageant family: Bob and Gerri Zettler, Sharon and Paul Herlihy, Dr. Banks, Dayna and Arlie Sowers, Jean and Sid Earhart, Noreen and Lloyd Young, John Kunkle, and Steven Oliveri.

Jim Outhouse, Jerry Baehr, and Susie Lee for the beautiful gowns and support.

Jackie Morris and family, and the town of Pickerington, Ohio.

Kim Vandervort and the town of Canton, Ohio.

The Ravenna Chamber of Commerce, Rick Coe and The Town of Ravenna.

The Town of Warren, The Town of Columbus

And every town across the beautiful state of Ohio that gifted me with their kindness and culture.

Randy Davilla of Hierophant Publishing for telling me I have three books in me and not just one. And...for telling me to get an agent.

Lastly, a huge thank you to Elizabeth R. Wyatt for the one minute rough sketch she did of me throwing off a crown. Yet another treasure I can add to the trove of framers and shared moments in our kitchen, where we riff on anything and everything.

HELLERTOWN AREA LIBRARY
409 Constitution Avenue
Hellertown, PA 18055
610-838-8381